the Ojibwa

People of the Great Lakes

by Anne M. Todd

Consultant:
Judy Lawrence
Media Specialist
Nay Ah Shing School
Mille Lacs Band of Ojibwa
Onamia, Minnesota

Bridgestone Books

an imprint of Capstone Press
Mankato, Minnesota

Bridgestone Books are published by Capstone Press
151 Good Counsel Drive, P.O. Box 669, Mankato, Minnesota 56002
http://www.capstone-press.com

Printed in the United States of America.

Library of Congress Cataloging-in-Publication Data
Todd, Anne M.
  Ojibwa: people of the Great Lakes / by Anne M. Todd.
    v. cm.—(American Indian nations)
  Includes bibliographical references and index.
  Contents: The Ojibwa—Life among the Ojibwa—Conflicts and
  culture—Life in a modern world—Sharing the old ways.
  ISBN 0-7368-1356-X (hardcover)
  1. Ojibwa Indians—History—Juvenile literature. 2. Ojibwa
  Indians—Social life and customs—Juvenile literature. [1. Ojibwa
  Indians. 2. Indians of North America—Great Lakes.] I. Title.
  II. American Indian nations series.
  E99.C6 T63 2003
  977.004'973—dc21   2002002654

Editorial Credits
Bradley P. Hoehn, editor; Kia Adams, designer and illustrator; Wanda Winch,
photo researcher; Karen Risch, product planning editor

Photo Credits
Unicorn Stock Photos/Phyllis Kedl, cover, Alice Prescott, 13; Corbis/Macduff
Everton, cover inset, Raymond Gehman, 18; Doranne Jacobson, 4, 42; Stock
Montage, Inc./The Newberry Library, 8, 10, 11, 22-23; Visuals Unlimited/David
Sieren, 14-15; Capstone Press/Gary Sundermeyer, 15 (recipe); North Wind
Picture Archives, 16, 24-25; Stock Montage, Inc., 20, 26-27, 28-29; Minnesota
Historical Society Museum Collections, 31, 44, 45; Mille Lacs Band of Ojibwe,
32, 38, 40-41; Cumberland County Historical Society, Carlisle, PA/A.A. Line,
34-35; Official Indian Health Service (IHS) photo, 37

1 2 3 4 5 6 07 06 05 04 03 02

Table of Contents

Features

Ojibwa celebrate their cultural heritage through events like powwows. This pair of Ojibwa wear traditional headdresses.

Chapter One

Who Are the Ojibwa?

The Ojibwa are a group of American Indians. They live in the upper woodlands in the Midwest of the United States. Ojibwa can also be spelled "Ojibway" or "Ojibwe."

The Ojibwa call themselves Anishinabe, which means "original people." This term refers to all native people living in North and South America, including the Ojibwa. When the Anishinabe came in contact with white settlers, the settlers mispronounced the word "Ojibwa." It sounded more like "Chippewa" when they said it. The white settlers referred to the Indians as Chippewa instead of Ojibwa. The U.S. government used the word Chippewa to refer to the Ojibwa in treaties and other legal agreements between the nations. Many Ojibwa elders and people of the tribe do not recognize the term Chippewa.

More than 120,000 Ojibwa people live in the United States today. Most live in an area that stretches from Montana to Michigan. There are 25 different Ojibwa tribes in this region. About 60,000 Ojibwa live in Canada. About half of Canadian Ojibwa live on reserves. A reserve is a Canadian reservation.

Most Ojibwa live in Minnesota, Wisconsin, and Michigan. Ojibwa reservations in Minnesota are located in the northern half of the state. A reservation is a piece of land the government sets aside for Indians. There are also Ojibwa reservations in Wisconsin and Michigan.

About half of the Ojibwa live all year-round on reservations, while the other half spend most of the year in large cities. In the city, Ojibwa seek better jobs and educational opportunities than the reservations offer. Most Ojibwa who leave the reservation return. They visit during the summer months to spend time with family and relatives. They also attend cultural events such as powwows.

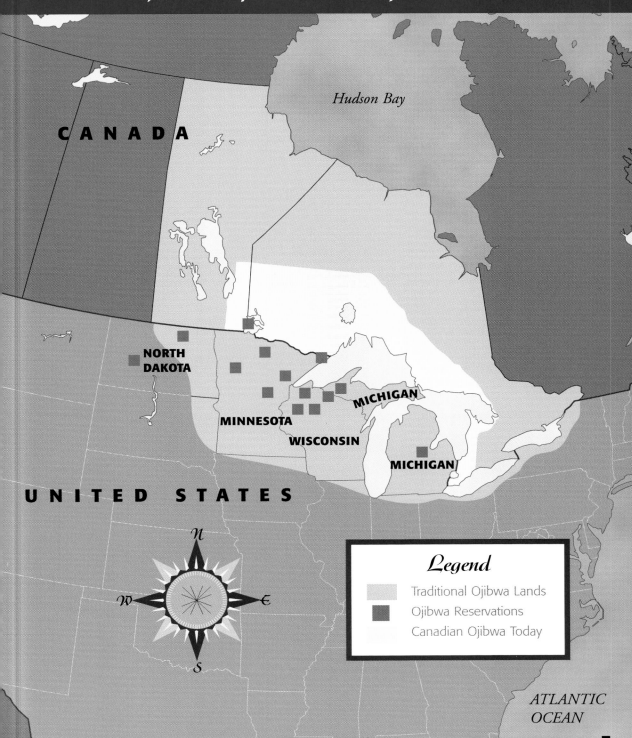

Hudson Bay

CANADA

NORTH
DAKOTA

MINNESOTA

WISCONSIN

MICHIGAN

MICHIGAN

UNITED STATES

N

W   E

S

Legend

Traditional Ojibwa Lands

Ojibwa Reservations

Canadian Ojibwa Today

*ATLANTIC
OCEAN*

7

In the 1840s, an Ojibwa village was located on the St. Mary River. The Ojibwa would live close to the river to be closer to the supply of fish.

Life among the Ojibwa

Before contact with whites, the Ojibwa lived primarily in woodlands. They hunted, fished, and grew wild rice.

The Ojibwa first lived from the East Coast to Hudson Bay. Around the year 1500, they moved west to the Great Lakes region, where many still live today.

The Yearly Cycle

In early spring, usually March or April, the Ojibwa made maple sugar. Each family, which included father, mother, children, grandparents, aunts, uncles, and cousins, had their own section within a maple forest.

The Ojibwa removed the sap from the maple trees. Sap is a sticky, sweet liquid that runs inside trees. Ojibwa cut gashes in the trees and placed containers made of birch bark under each gash to collect the syrup. This process is called tapping.

The Ojibwa then boiled the sap. Boiling turns sap into syrup. The Ojibwa stirred the syrup with a paddle until the syrup turned into a sugar. They sometimes poured the syrup into a mold to form a sugar cake.

In the summer, while men hunted and fished, women and children collected berries. They picked blueberries,

Ojibwa made camps in the woods to harvest the maple syrup needed for sugar.

Wild rice was collected in canoes. One person steered while the others beat the stalks of rice over the canoe so that the wild rice would fall into the canoe.

chokecherries, and juneberries. They brought them back to camp and laid them in the sun to dry. The dried berries could be stored and eaten the following winter.

In the fall, the Ojibwa gathered manomin, or wild rice. Manomin grows in lakes and rivers. Ojibwa legend says the Great Spirit gave manomin as a gift to the Ojibwa.

When it was time to gather the wild rice in the fall, two or three people rode in a canoe. One person steered and the others harvested the rice, collecting it using two sticks. Each stick was about 24 inches (61 centimeters) long.

The Ojibwa used one stick to bend the rice stacks over the boat. They knocked the ripe rice kernels into the canoe with the other stick. When the boat was full, the Ojibwa took the rice to the shore and laid it to dry on sheets of birch bark.

During the winter months, the Ojibwa had many duties. The men and boys hunted and trapped animals. In the evenings, elders told stories around the fire. The Ojibwa ate food they had gathered. They preserved and stored foods gathered during the previous summer for winter. They also ate fresh venison, or deer meat, that the hunters shot. The men fixed their bows and arrows and the women sewed during the winter. The Ojibwa prepared for maple sugaring, which would take place again in the spring.

Wigwams

The Ojibwa lived in dwellings called wigwams. To make a wigwam, they first made a frame of poles. They then covered the frame with heavy mats made out of bulrush, a kind of bark. Some wigwams were round while others were oval. A blanket usually covered the doorway.

Two or three families might live in a 12 foot by 10 foot (3.7 meter by 3.0 meter) wigwam. In large wigwams, more than one fire might be burning. Above each fire was an opening in the top of the wigwam to let out smoke.

The Ojibwa made wigwams from pole frames covered with bulrush. A blanket usually covered the doorway.

Families slept on thin feather beds on top of cedar branches. Women filled deer hide mattresses with duck feathers to make the feather beds. They made blankets from deer or bear hide that was tanned with the fur still on them. When the bedding was not in use, it was rolled up and placed along the edges of the wigwam. The rolls then could be used as seats. Women tanned hides by hanging them on a bush. There they dried in the sun for a few days. Women could also stretch the hide on a frame and leave it to dry in the sun.

Family Roles

Ojibwa infants spent most of their first year of life in cradleboards. A cradleboard is a board of wood on which a baby lies. Leather straps hold the baby in place. A piece of wood at the bottom holds the baby's feet in place. The mother placed soft moss around the baby to keep the infant warm and comfortable.

Women spent a great deal of time with their babies. Mothers sang lullabies, quieted babies when they grew fussy, and kept their babies near them while they worked. Grandmothers often gave advice to mothers on how to raise the babies.

Children spent their days watching and learning from their parents and grandparents. Children collected plants,

Popped Wild Rice

Wild rice was an important food for the Ojibwa people. Before they had contact with white people, Ojibwa used animal fat for cooking instead of corn or vegetable oil. They cooked wild rice in fat until it popped, somewhat like popcorn. Instead of butter and salt, Ojibwas flavored this popped treat with maple sugar or maple syrup. You may want to add butter and salt for a tastier treat.

Ingredients:

2 tablespoons (30 mL) corn oil or vegetable oil
1 cup (250 mL) uncooked wild rice
¼ cup (50 mL) melted butter
2 tablespoons (30 mL) pure maple syrup or maple sugar
salt (to taste)

Equipment:

12-inch (30-centimeter) skillet
large bowl
measuring spoons
dry-ingredient measuring cups

What you do:

1. With an adult to supervise, place 1 tablespoon (15 mL) oil in skillet.
2. Heat skillet on stove over medium heat.
3. Add ½ cup (125 mL) wild rice to oil in skillet.
4. Swish skillet over the stove burner to keep the rice from sticking until the kernels pop.
5. Pour popped kernels into the bowl.
6. Repeat steps 3 through 5.
7. Pour butter and maple syrup (or maple sugar) over popped rice.
8. Gently toss rice kernels in bowl to evenly coat them.
9. Sprinkle with salt to taste.

Makes about 2 to 3 cups (500 to 750 mL) popped rice kernels.

Ojibwa would often bow hunt for deer at night. Bow hunting
was a very important skill to learn.

brought them home, and dried them in the sun. They then crushed the dried plants to make a refreshing drink. Parents and elders taught them which plants could make a drink, which could be used as medicine, and which to leave alone.

Girls learned many things from their mothers. They began chopping and carrying wood at an early age. Mothers taught daughters to cook and sew. They learned to make miniature wigwams and played with these toys when their work was done. Girls played with dolls made from pine needles and tree bark.

The women in the village tanned animal hides, cooked meals, and set up wigwams. They gathered sap for maple sugar in the spring and gathered wild rice in the fall. During the summer months, they spent a great deal of time drying and storing food.

Boys learned from their fathers how to shoot arrows with a bow. This skill was important for hunters and warriors. Boys began learning to shoot at about age 5. They also played games and learned to fish. They spent many hours swimming and running races.

The men in the village hunted game such as deer, moose, fox, and wolves. Men hunted with bows and arrows, but also hunted using traps. They used the stalks of nettle plants to make nets and boards for the traps. Ojibwa men trapped deer, otters, beavers, minks, fish, rabbits, bears, and birds.

Religious Beliefs and Ceremonies

Ojibwa believed Gitchi-Manito, or the Great Spirit, made rock, fire, wind, and water. From these four elements Gitchi-Manito created the Earth, Sun, and everything else.

Ojibwa painted stories of their religious beliefs on cave walls. This Ojibwa petroglyph shows the figure of a man with two animals. Ojibwa believed all creatures had spirits.

The Ojibwa believed that everything, including people, plants, animals, and rocks, has a spirit. If an Ojibwa took something, such as a deer to eat, that person would leave an offering of tobacco. They left it where the deer was killed as a sign of respect to the Gitchi-Manito.

The Ojibwa performed a naming ceremony after a child was born. The parents chose a special person to name the child. The namer often was a close friend of the family or a member of the tribe known to be a wise person.

The namer spent time getting to know the child. The namer would then go in to the forest and meditate, thinking quietly to keep the mind and spirit clear. At this time, the namer waited for a vision, or dream. The vision helped the person choose a name for the child. For instance, if the person had a vision of a flying eagle, the child would be called Flying Eagle. The namer collected plants, put them in a medicine bag and presented it to the child at the ceremony.

The family prepared a great feast with much food for the naming ceremony. People from the village attended the ceremony and brought gifts for the baby. At the ceremony, the namer announced the name of the child. This ceremony honored not only the baby, but also Gitchi-Manito.

Hudson's Bay Trading Company was a very important store for the Ojibwa. They traded furs and animal skins for items such as cooking pots, blankets, and guns.

Chapter Three

Conflicts and Culture

The Ojibwa first came in contact with white people in the early 1600s. At this time, the Ojibwa lived primarily on the northern shore of Lake Huron. French traders had come to the Great Lakes area for animal furs. The Ojibwa received gifts such as cookware, knives, sewing needles, blankets, and guns, in exchange for furs. By the late 1600s, many young French fur traders married Ojibwa women. These men were welcomed into the tribe. The children of these couples were called Métis.

For the most part, the relationship between the Ojibwa and the French was a good one. The French fur traders respected the Ojibwa way of life, their customs, and their beliefs. They did not try to force French values and customs on the Ojibwa.

Pushing West

There were several American Indian tribes that lived near the Ojibwa. The Ojibwa had enemies on both sides of them. The Iroquois lived in the east. The Lakota lived in the west. Nearby tribes that were friendly to the Ojibwa included the Ottawa and the Potawatomi (POT-uh-WOT-uh-mee). All three of these tribes spoke similar languages. They frequently traded with each other for items they needed.

The Iroquois moved into the Great Lakes region to try to take over hunting and trading grounds from the Ojibwa and the Ottawa. The Ojibwa had a number of battles with a band of Iroquois. In 1662, the Ojibwa finally wiped out their camp during a battle. The Ojibwa began to expand to the West. They also began moving west along the southern shore of Lake Superior into present-day Wisconsin.

Trade Competition

In 1680, a new group of fur traders entered the Hudson Bay area. The British built the Hudson's Bay Company. French fur traders now had competition. Both groups wanted American Indian tribes to hunt and trap animals for them. The competition created tension between both the French and British traders and the American Indian tribes.

Ojibwa warriors would fight to expand their lands. They would fight other Indian tribes for their territory and forced the Sioux from what is now northern Minnesota.

During all this competition, Indian tribes and Europeans trapped large numbers of furs. The prices of furs began to drop. In 1698, the French government stopped all trade at its western trading posts. Western Indians, including the Ottawa and some Ojibwa, no longer had a trading post nearby.

The nearest trading post was on the other side of Iroquois territory. The Iroquois were enemies of the Ojibwa. In 1701, 15 Indian nations signed an agreement allowing Ottawa Indians to pass through Iroquois hunting grounds to reach a British trading post.

The Ojibwa had grown dependent on the white people's supplies. They became friendly with the Ottawa. The Ojibwa were able to receive the trade goods they needed from the Ottawa. The Ojibwa were also able to get supplies through the British trading post.

In the 1700s, the Ojibwa continued to make strong trade partners. They also searched for new hunting grounds. Some Ojibwa began to explore the southern part of present-day Michigan. Other bands were entering the upper area of present-day Minnesota. Lakota Indians also lived in Minnesota.

Also in the 1700s, the Lakota and Dakota began to attack French fur traders. The Ojibwa wanted to trade goods with

the French. The Ojibwa began to fight the Lakota and Dakota to stop them from chasing away the French traders. Over the next hundred years, they pushed the Lakota west out of both present-day Wisconsin and present-day Minnesota. They pushed the Dakota into southern Minnesota.

When the French stopped all trade at western trading posts, some Ojibwa had to pass through enemy territory to reach a British trading post.

The French and Indian War

Trade wars continued between the French and British. The Ojibwa, Ottawa, Delaware, and Shawnee tribes all sided with the French. In 1752, Charles de Langlade led an attack that destroyed an English trading post in present-day Ohio. A few years later, an Ojibwa leader named Wasson helped defeat a

Pontiac was a Ottawa Indian Chief. Pontiac led the rebellion against the British forts.

British general in Pennsylvania. This battle was one that led to the French and Indian War (1754–1763).

In 1759, the British defeated the French in Quebec. Later, French-controlled Montreal surrendered to the British. French rule in North America came to an end. Great Britain took control of the land France once owned. This area included the land east of the Mississippi River and territory in Canada.

Pontiac's Rebellion and the Revolutionary War

Unlike the French, the British did not get along with the Ojibwa. The British did not try to understand the Ojibwa culture. They did not allow Indians to charge trade goods.

An Ottawa leader named Pontiac led a rebellion against the British. Ojibwa warriors helped Pontiac take over British forts. When Pontiac needed help fighting the British, he turned to the French. But the French said they were through fighting the British. Pontiac tried to fight on without help, but he finally signed a peace treaty with the British in 1766.

In 1768, the British agreed to the Treaty of Fort Stanwix. The terms stated that the land west of the Ohio River was Indian country. White settlers could not enter that area.

The boundaries in the Treaty of Fort Stanwix often were ignored. White settlers continued to move into Indian country. Wars between whites and Indians became more frequent. After the Revolutionary War (1775–1783), even more settlers moved into Indian country.

Pontiac met with Major Henry Gladwyn to discuss the Treaty of Fort Stanwix. The British agreed to the treaty as a result of Pontiac's Rebellion.

In 1795, Ojibwa and other Indian tribes met to discuss and sign the Greensville Treaty. This treaty forced the Indians to give up the southern two-thirds of Ohio to the U.S. government. This area then was available for settlers to occupy. The treaty also stated that the U.S. government would build 16 forts between the Ohio River and the Mississippi River.

Bureau of Indian Affairs

The Sioux and the Ojibwa were fighting over their boundaries. In 1825, the Bureau of Indian Affairs (BIA) organized a council in Prairie du Chien, Wisconsin. The BIA is a federal agency involved with trade and Indian relations. At the Prairie du Chien council, BIA members wanted to end the conflict between the Dakota Sioux Nation (called the Sioux in the treaty) and the Ojibwa. The treaty called for peace between these tribes. It also determined a boundary tribes could cross only if they were peaceful.

Negotiations continued in 1826 for the Treaty of Fond du Lac. Several bands of Ojibwa had not attended the first treaty signing. One article in this new treaty called for the United States to pay $1,000 each year to build a school on Ojibwa land. This school was the first in Michigan territory for Ojibwa children.

Reservations

Over the next 100 years, the U.S. government began a series of treaties with the Ojibwa. These treaties placed Ojibwa people onto reservations, mainly in Minnesota, Wisconsin, and Michigan. With each treaty the government promised the Ojibwa would receive annual shipments of food and supplies. These shipments were often late and the food often arrived spoiled or rotten. Many times the shipments would not arrive at all.

One purpose of reservations was to confine Indians to one area. Another purpose was to "civilize" them. The BIA hoped to change the Ojibwa's way of life to be more like European Americans. BIA officials wanted the Ojibwa to work on farms, live in houses, and go to Christian churches.

With limited hunting and fishing grounds, the Ojibwa had little choice but to turn to farming. Reservation land often contained poor soil. The Ojibwa had little farm equipment, and little desire to follow the ways of the whites. Many Ojibwa faced poverty and starvation on the reservation. The Ojibwa standard of living grew much worse.

World War II

During World War II (1939–1945), many Ojibwa served in the U.S. Army. Others aided the war effort by taking jobs in

William Whipple Warren

William Whipple Warren was born in 1825. His mother was Ojibwa and his father was a descendant from a Mayflower pilgrim. Warren was a native speaker of Ojibwa, but also learned to speak English fluently. He attended schools on the East Coast under white teachers.

When Warren returned home, he spent a great deal of time documenting Ojibwa stories and traditional customs. His writings were later published in a book called *History of the Ojibway People*. This book was the first to document the Ojibwa people by a native author. Warren died at the young age of 28 from tuberculosis, a disease that destroys the lungs.

factories and shipyards. Some Ojibwa worked construction jobs in Alaska and Newfoundland, Canada. Moving away from the reservation gave these Ojibwa more money and a higher standard of living.

Ojibwa children attend reservation schools where they learn computer skills and other subjects such as math, reading, and science. They also learn about their heritage.

Chapter Four

Life in a Modern World

Most Ojibwa live in the Great Lakes region of the United States and Canada. About half of the Ojibwa people live in cities and towns away from reservations.

No matter where they live, Ojibwa children share many of the same experiences as other American children. They wear T-shirts and blue jeans, go to movies and video arcades, search the Internet, go shopping, and spend time with their friends. But they also might attend a weekend powwow, listen to traditional Ojibwa stories, and learn the Ojibwa language.

Education and Healthcare

Between 1900 and 1970, white people forced many Ojibwa children to attend boarding schools. The children were not allowed to visit their families while they lived at the school. They were not allowed to speak their native language. If they did, they risked physical punishment. They could not practice their religion or hold traditional ceremonies. The children had to learn to read and write English. They had to take on English names, practice Christianity, and learn history recorded by white people.

Many changes have been made in American Indian education since 1970. The Ojibwa have spent millions of dollars building new elementary schools, middle schools, high schools, and colleges. Children and young adults now learn the Ojibwa language, history, and culture in school.

Each year, more and more Ojibwa leave the reservation to seek education in cities. Large numbers of Ojibwa attend colleges such as the University of Minnesota and the University of Michigan. Some large universities teach native languages such as Ojibwa and Dakota.

In the early 1900s, health conditions on Ojibwa reservations were poor. Tuberculosis, a disease of the lungs, and trachoma, a disease of the eye, once were common among the Ojibwa. Diabetes, a disease in which there is too much

sugar in the blood, was also very common. Today, more money is spent to educate people about preventing disease. The reservations also are building better medical facilities.

Girls at the Carlisle Indian School in Carlisle, Pennsylvania, lived at the boarding school and studied in their rooms. This picture was taken in 1910.

Economics

Today, the Ojibwa are able to bring in great amounts of money for their tribe through Indian gaming operations such as casinos. Ojibwa casinos operate in North Dakota, Minnesota, Wisconsin, and Michigan. Both native and non-native people come to the casinos.

Tribal members have worked hard to improve reservation life. They have built tribal centers that oversee reservation housing, health care, and education. Tribal members are working to increase the number of jobs on reservations. This effort helps to raise the standard of living for the Ojibwa.

Politics

Minnesota has seven Ojibwa reservations. Except for the Red Lake Reservation, these reservations follow one tribal government. People from these six reservations form the Minnesota Chippewa Tribe.

People elect a tribal council as well as a tribal chairman. The tribal chairman and council govern the Minnesota Chippewa Tribe. The Ojibwa government passes laws and finds ways to improve the standard of living for its people. Red Lake reservation has its own tribal government.

Dr. Kathleen Annette

Dr. Kathleen Annette is the first Minnesota Ojibwa woman to become a medical doctor. She is the director of Bemidji Area Indian Health Service. Dr. Annette is a member of the White Earth Reservation and has strong ties to both the Red Lake and Leech Lake Reservations. She was raised on the Red Lake Reservation and practiced medicine at the Leech Lake Reservation.

She manages a health care program that serves 91,000 American Indians. The majority of these programs are located on 35 reservations and in five urban areas.

Dr. Annette is a highly respected American Indian leader. She gives lectures to medical schools on Indian health concerns and issues. She has received many awards for her commitment to Indian people. She received the U.S. Public Health Service Outstanding Service Award in 1993, and the Presidential Award in the year 2000.

Ojibwa children learn from all members of the community. They learn about their cultural heritage through family, friends, teachers, and elders.

Chapter Five

Sharing the Old Ways

The Ojibwa are ensuring a future of
educated children by building new schools
on the reservations. Reservation children
now can learn about their history, culture,
and the traditions of their ancestors.
Reservation schools offer classes that use
computers to help children prepare for
good-paying jobs.

Ceremonial dances play an important part at traditional
gatherings, such as powwows.

are present in almost every large American city. At the cultural centers, young people learn about a particular tribe's history and traditions. American Indian authors and artists sell books and artwork in the center's store. Elders come to the center to teach classes about crafts or language. Young and old people alike gather to share their stories and experiences.

Powwows

Powwows are important to preserving traditional Ojibwa culture. A powwow is a gathering that lasts two to four days. A variety of events take place during this time. People perform ceremonies, and dancers compete for prizes. Children and adults ride or perform in parades, and everyone is able to taste a variety of traditional foods.

Dancing has been a part of Ojibwa culture from the beginning. Long ago, they might have made a costume from rabbit hides. The dancer would then dance, using movements that looked like a rabbit. Today, this activity is called traditional dancing.

Other kinds of dancing also are performed at powwows, including fancy-shawl dancing, gourd dancing, and jingle-dress dancing.

Ojibwa Timeline

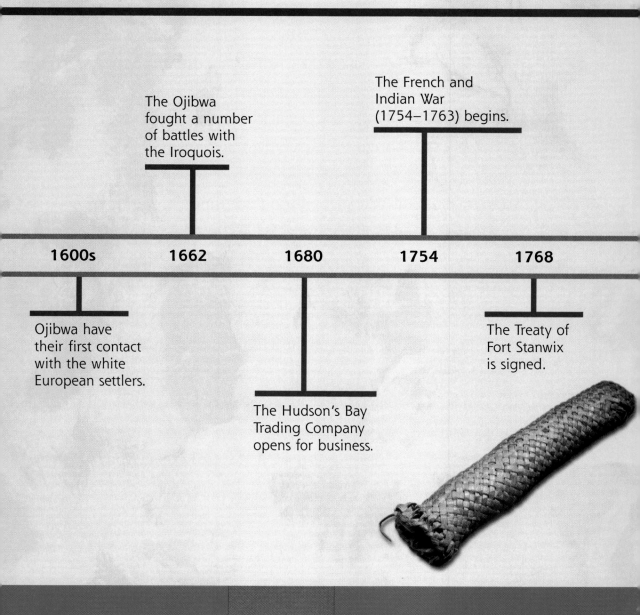

The Ojibwa fought a number of battles with the Iroquois.

The French and Indian War (1754–1763) begins.

1600s   **1662**   **1680**   **1754**   **1768**

Ojibwa have their first contact with the white European settlers.

The Treaty of Fort Stanwix is signed.

The Hudson's Bay Trading Company opens for business.

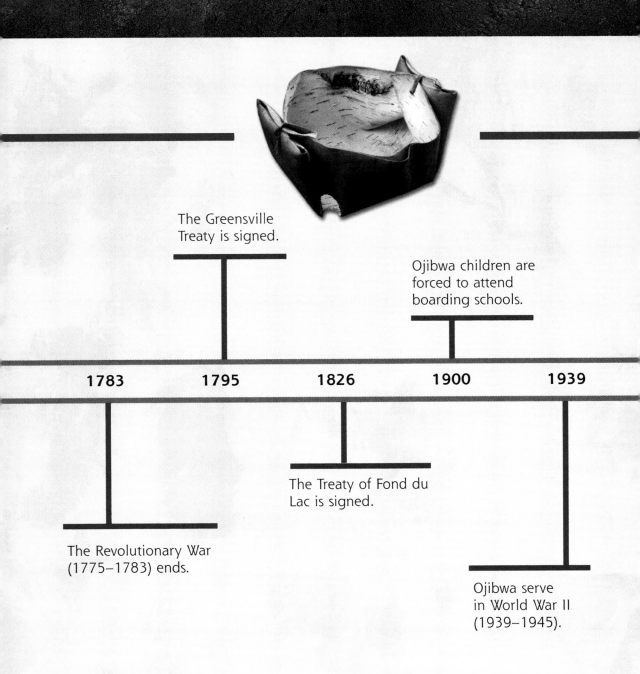

The Greensville
Treaty is signed.

Ojibwa children are
forced to attend
boarding schools.

1783   **1795**   **1826**   **1900**   **1939**

The Treaty of Fond du
Lac is signed.

The Revolutionary War
(1775–1783) ends.

Ojibwa serve
in World War II
(1939–1945).

Glossary

ancestor (AN-sess-tur)—a member of a person's family who lived a long time ago

Anishinabe (ah-nish-ih-NAH-bay)—Ojibwa word meaning original people

band (BAND)—a group of people smaller than a tribe

manomin (mah-NO-men)—Ojibwa word meaning wild rice

nation (NAY-shun)—a tribe, or a group of people who live in the same area and speak the same language

reservation (rez-er-VAY-shun)—an area of land set aside for American Indians by the U.S. government

sacred (SAY-kred)—highly valued and important

trachoma (tra-KOH-muh)—a bacterial eye infection that may cause blindness

treaty (TREE-tee)—a legal agreement between nations

tuberculosis (tu-bur-kyuh-LOH-siss) —a highly contagious bacterial disease that usually destroys the lungs

For Further Reading

Bial, Raymond. *The Ojibwe.* Lifeways. New York: Benchmark Books, 2000

Lund, Bill. *The Ojibwa Indians.* Native Peoples. Mankato, MN: Bridgestone Books, 1997

McCarthy, Cathy. *The Ojibwa.* Indian Nations. Austin, Texas: Raintree Steck-Vaughn, 2000

Places to Write and Visit

Anishinaabe Cultural Center and Gallery
921 Eighth Street SE
Detroit Lakes, MN 56501

Minneapolis American Indian Center
1800 East Franklin Avenue
Minneapolis, MN 55404

Minnesota Historical Society
345 West Kellogg Boulevard
St. Paul, MN 55102

Internet Sites

Anishinabe Experience
http://www.anishexp.com

Chippewa/Ojibway/Anishinabe Literature
http://www.indians.org/welker/chippewa.htm

Ojibwa History
http://www.tolatsga.org/ojib.html

Index